THE 12 ZEERBEEZ
(volume 1)

ABOUT THE AUTHOR

My name is Jesse Sahbi, a cartoonist born in Cote d'Ivoire. I've been cartooning since 1980 as a political cartoonist in Cote d'Ivoire's first daily newspaper called Fraternit Matin from 1980 to 2001, and in many other magazines from West Africa and France. I won a cartoon award in 1989 at Biarritz in France.

I've had a lot of interviews on national radio in several West African countries for my cartoon character Zeerbeez, including BBC Radio in London. I'm also an artist, musician, singer, and composer, and I've toured in several cities in West Africa and in the US.

Zerkisbudinetown

(*) LANGUAGE GOURO FROM CÔTE D'IVOIRE.

(*) LANGUAGE GOURO FROM CÔTE D'IVOIRE.

(*) LANGUAGE GOURO FROM CÔTE D'IVOIRE.

(*) LANGUAGE GOURO FROM CÔTE D'IVOIRE.

(*) LANGUAGE GOURO FROM CÔTE D'IVOIRE.

(*) LANGUAGE GOURO FROM CÔTE D'IVOIRE.

(*) LANGUAGE GOURO FROM CÔTE D'IVOIRE.

(*) LANGUAGE GOURO FROM CÔTE D'IVOIRE.

TO BE CONTINUED.

THE 12 ZEERBEEZ
WORLD CHAMPS 2026

(volume 2)

(*) LANGUAGE GOURO FROM CÔTE D'IVOIRE.

(*) LANGUAGE GOURO FROM CÔTE D'IVOIRE.

(*) Language Gouro from Côte d'Ivoire.

(*) Language Gouro from Côte d'Ivoire.

(*) LANGUAGE GOURO FROM CÔTE D'IVOIRE.

(*) LANGUAGE GOURO FROM CÔTE D'IVOIRE.

(*) LANGUAGE GOURO FROM CÔTE D'IVOIRE.

(*) LANGUAGE GOURO FROM CÔTE D'IVOIRE.

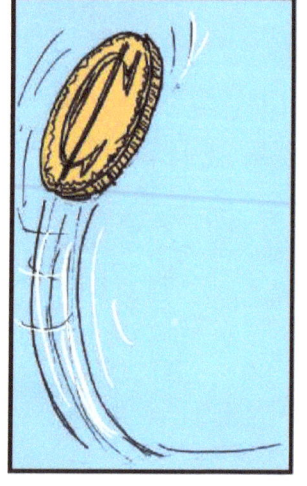

(*) LANGUAGE GOURO FROM CÔTE D'IVOIRE.

(*) LANGUAGE GOURO FROM CÔTE D'IVOIRE.

(*) BOA BOA ZIRIGBI KA WIZI VOALO.

NO NO ZEERBEEZ DOESN'T RETALIATE.

LET OUT ALL THE COBRAAAS!

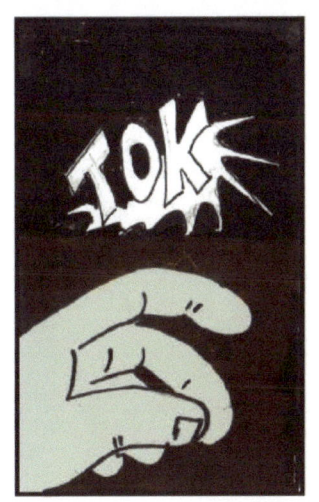

(*) LANGUAGE GOURO FROM CÔTE D'IVOIRE.

END

THE 12 ZEERBEEZ COLLECTION

NEXT

HOW TARIFFS STARTED AND ENDED UP

www.ingramcontent.com/pod-product-compliance
Lightning Source LLC
Chambersburg PA
CBHW042054050526
44107CB00109B/1124